Cute animals Grayscale

I0408846

coloring book for adults relaxation

New way to color with Grayscale coloring book

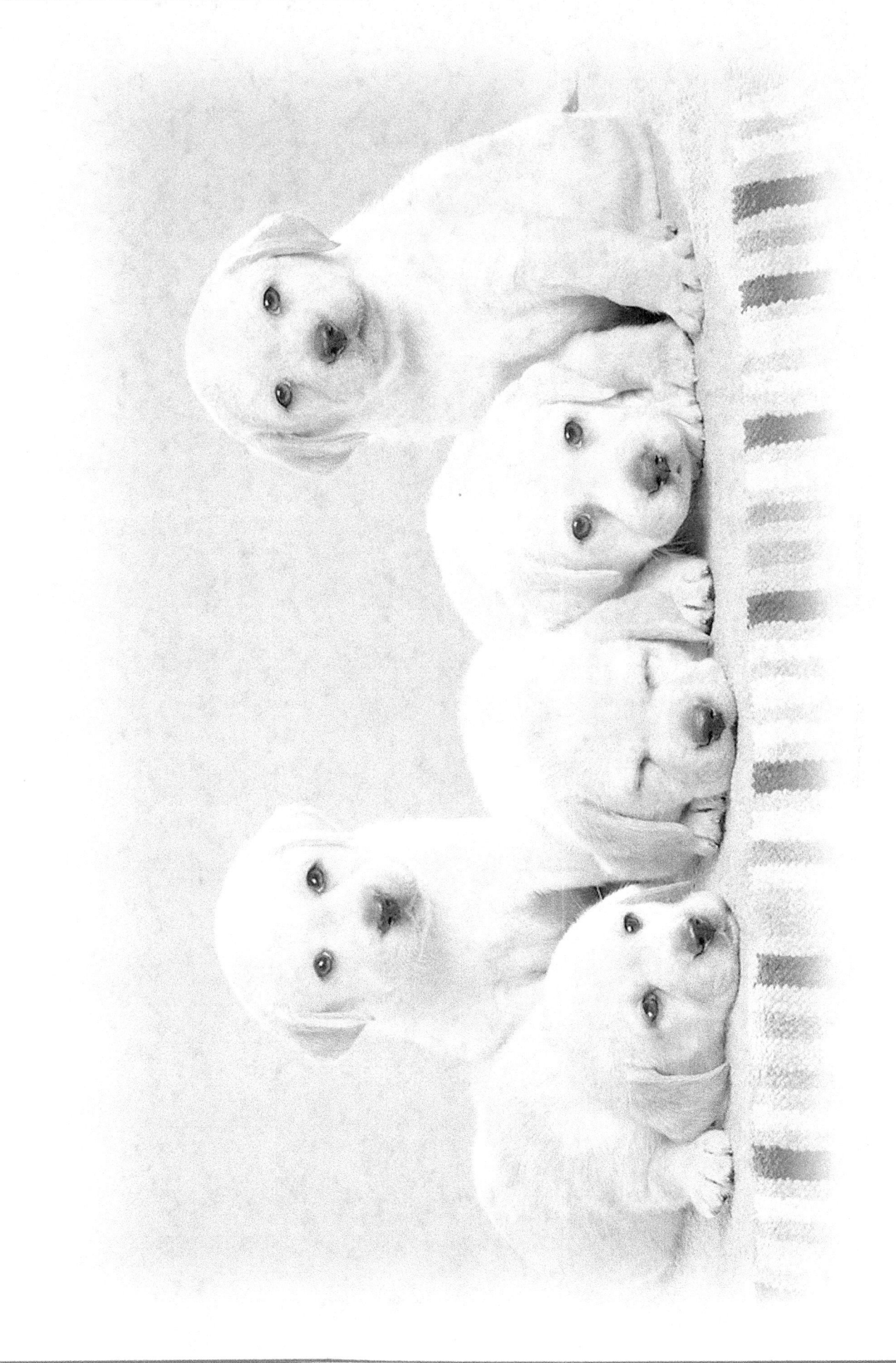

Your Amazon Review could really help us.
Thank you for your support.

Use Below Link to access review of this book.

http://bit.ly/a_grayscale__review_1

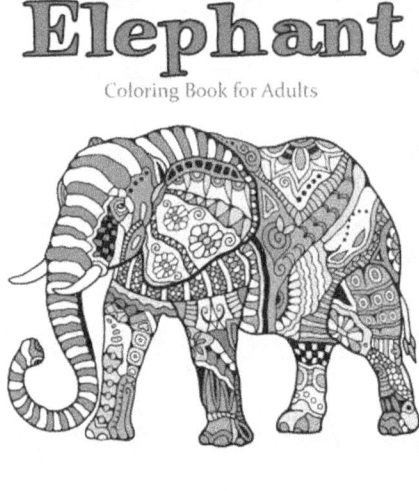

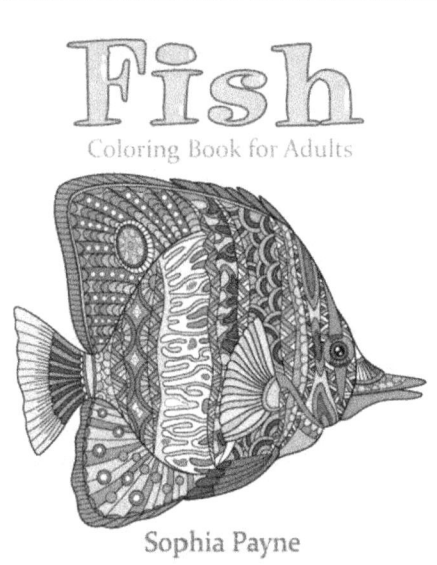

Join Us >> bit.ly/get_sample_free

- Get Free "Reviw Copies" of our New releases
- Exclusive offers and book giveaways
- More events from our community

Thank you